BASEBALL'S

NEW

WAVE

THE YOUNG SUPERSTARS
TAKING OVER THE GAME

JACE FREDERICK

First Edition
Third Printing, 2019

Book design by Sarah Taplin
Cover design by Sarah Taplin
Photographs ©: Julie Jacobson/AP Images, cover (left), 1 (left), back cover, 102; Mark J. Terrill/AP Images, cover (center), 1 (center); Leslie Plaza Johnson/Icon Sportswire/AP Images, cover (right), 1 (right), 40; Curtis Compton/Atlanta Journal-Constitution/AP, 4, 121 (top right); John Minchillo/AP Images, 10; Brian Rothmuller/Icon Sportswire, 12, 14, 121 (top center); Mark Goldman/Icon Sportswire/AP Images, 18, 78; Fred Thornhill/The Canadian Press/AP Images, 24; David J. Phillip/AP Images, 26, 31; Ian Johnson/Icon Sportswire/AP Images, 34; Eric Gay/AP Images, 45, 121 (top left); Cliff Welch/Icon Sportswire/AP Images, 48; Kathy Willens/AP Images, 53, 58; Tomasso DeRosa/AP Images, 61; Tony Dejak/AP Images, 66, 94–95; Carlos Osorio/AP Images, 69; Joshua Lavallee/Icon Sportswire, 74; Kyodo/AP Images, 82, 104; Jae C. Hong/AP Images, 86, 121 (bottom); Nick Wosika/Icon Sportswire/AP Images, 90; Duane Burleson/AP Images, 98; Adam Davis/Icon Sportswire/AP Images, 109; Kyusung Gong/AP Images, 112; Ted S. Warren/AP Images, 116

Design Elements ©: Shutterstock

Press Box Books, an imprint of Press Room Editions.

Library of Congress Control Number: 2018952201

ISBN
978-1-63494-052-8 (paperback)
978-1-63494-064-1 (epub)
978-1-63494-076-4 (hosted ebook)

Distributed by North Star Editions, Inc.
2297 Waters Drive
Mendota Heights, MN 55120
www.northstareditions.com
Printed in the United States of America

TABLE OF CONTENTS

CHAPTER 1

RONALD ACUÑA JR.

Few players were more popular with Atlanta Braves fans than Chipper Jones. So when Jones was asked about Ronald Acuña Jr., the team's 20-year-old left fielder, during spring training of 2018, people listened.

"He's as good a prospect as I've seen," Jones said.

It did not take long to see what all the excitement was about. Just one week into his Major League Baseball (MLB) career, the 6-foot, 180-pound Venezuelan prospect had proved he belonged. Debuting in April 2018, Acuña produced 13 hits in his first eight games, including five doubles and two home runs. He became the first player in Braves history to tally five extra-base hits in his first five games. By season's end, the player who was barely known just one season earlier was the league's Rookie of the Year.

Though not considered a top prospect, Ronald Acuña Jr. proved to be a big star for the Atlanta Braves.

Scouted as early as 14 years old, Acuña signed with the Braves for $100,000 in 2014. That was a modest figure compared with the game's most sought-after young international players. And even one year before his MLB debut, Acuña remained relatively unknown. When MLB Pipeline came out with its Top 100 Prospects lists in 2017, the young Venezuelan was nowhere to be found.

The lack of expectations created a lack of pressure that Acuña seems to savor.

"When I signed I wasn't really considered a highly touted prospect, so now it's even better," he said in 2018. "I feel the same way—I've never really had that pressure."

Acuña opened the 2017 season at the Class-A Advanced level. That is three steps below the major leagues. By the end of the year, he was obliterating Triple-A pitching and was widely considered one of the best prospects in baseball.

Prospect tools are graded on a 20 to 80 scale, with a 20 being the worst and 80 the best. A grade of 60 or higher is considered above average. Acuña entered the majors with all five tools—hitting for average, hitting for power, running, throwing, and fielding—rated at

60 or higher. Those tools were on full display in 2017. Acuña hit .325 with 21 home runs and 82 runs batted in (RBIs) to go with 44 stolen bases in 139 games played across three minor league levels.

> **"(ACUÑA) IS A BETTER ATHLETE THAN EVERYBODY ELSE. IT'S PRETTY HARD TO EXPLAIN. WHEN YOU WATCH HIM, YOU CAN JUST TELL THERE IS A DIFFERENCE."**
>
> **–DANSBY SWANSON, BRAVES SHORTSTOP**

"(Acuña) is a better athlete than everybody else," Braves shortstop Dansby Swanson said. "It's pretty hard to explain. When you watch him, you can just tell there is a difference. Whether you know a lot about baseball or know nothing, you can see that guy is doing something right."

Acuña has strong baseball bloodlines. His uncle, Jose Escobar, and many of his cousins reached the big leagues. His grandfather played minor league baseball. So did his father, Ronald Acuña Sr. The elder Acuña swears he had the talent to make it to the major leagues. Instead, he bounced around various minor league levels, never advancing past Double-A.

That hasn't been a problem with Acuña Jr., who his father said was "more talented and disciplined than I ever was." Acuña Jr. also had the benefit of coming from a family filled with pro baseball players.

"He was born with talent," Acuña Sr. said. "But the little things that you do to polish that talent, he learned from all of us."

Mentorship has played a large role in Acuña's rise. Playing a spring training game in 2018 against the Detroit Tigers, Acuña reached first base on a single. While there he started talking to Tigers first baseman Miguel Cabrera. Also from Venezuela, Cabrera grew up approximately two hours away from Acuña's

AIR ACUÑA

While in Triple-A, Acuña hit a home run in each of the first two games of a series. Prior to the third game, teammate Rio Ruiz issued Acuña a challenge. If Acuña, the leadoff hitter, opened the game with a home run, Ruiz would buy him a pair of Air Jordans. Challenge accepted. And Acuña indeed crushed the first pitch of the game out of the park. Ruiz delivered on his promise, giving Acuña a pair of black and white Jordans, size 11½. "There's nothing not special about him," Ruiz said.

hometown of La Guaira. Acuña had watched Cabrera as a child and still admires him to this day.

"We've always kind of had that relationship," Acuña said. "He just kind of gave me advice on all the small things and all the little things to do, especially once you get to the big leagues. The things you need to make sure you take care of and the things you do well and do right, things that will sustain your career as you move forward in the big leagues."

It doesn't take much knowledge of the game to be impressed by the way the ball jumps off Acuña's bat. Just ask Cincinnati Reds pitcher Homer Bailey. In the second inning of his second career game, Acuña took Bailey yard. He launched a slider four rows deep into the upper deck at the Great American Ball Park in Cincinnati.

Acuña's first major league home run traveled an estimated 416 feet, leaving the bat at a speed of 105.8 miles per hour. He ended the season with a .293 batting average and 26 homers.

"The ball explodes off his bat," Jones said. "He's got a great bat path. His bat is in the (hitting) zone a long time. You can't teach that. It's God given. Whoever taught him (did) very well."

Acuña blasts a home run for his second major league hit in April 2018.

It's when Acuña puts the bat on the ball that the real fun begins. Few can match Acuña's speed on the base paths. That showed during his major league debut. Acuña found himself on first base with the Braves trailing the Reds 4–3 in the eighth. Then, on a sharp single to left field, Acuña made it all the way to third. It took him 5.81 seconds to take two bases. Acuña went on to score the tying run as the Braves won 5–4.

"There's no fear at all on the base paths," Braves manager Brian Snitker said.

Acuña is one of the few players fast enough to cover 30-plus feet per second on the base paths. With his speed and his swing, it's no wonder he shot onto the major league scene so quickly. And he's done it all with a smile on his face. Acuña said he's always admired Jose Reyes. The New York Mets veteran always seems to have fun while playing at a high level. That's something Acuña has tried to do, too. It shows.

"I get the feeling that that kid just likes playing baseball," Snitker said. "He has fun on the baseball field, it doesn't matter where he is."

RONALD ACUÑA AT-A-GLANCE

BIRTHPLACE: La Guaira, Venezuela

BIRTH DATE: December 18, 1997

POSITION: Left fielder

BATS: Right

THROWS: Right

SIZE: 6', 180 pounds

TEAM: Atlanta Braves

MAJOR LEAGUE DEBUT: April 25, 2018 (vs. the Cincinnati Reds)

SIGNED AS AN INTERNATIONAL FREE AGENT BY THE BRAVES IN 2014

CHAPTER 2

OZZIE ALBIES

Atlanta Braves pitcher Lucas Sims's first thought when he first saw Ozzie Albies at an instructional was a common one.

"Who's this little guy?" Sims recalled.

By now, Sims knows. Everyone does.

Little? Yes. Albies, the Braves second baseman, stands at just 5 feet, 8 inches and weighs 165 pounds. But his game is large.

Born in Willemstad, Curacao, Albies is on his way to being the next Braves star from the Caribbean island nation. He's following in the footsteps of players such as Andruw Jones, Jair Jurrjens, and Andrelton Simmons. The Braves scout Curacao closely. There's a reason for that.

In 2018, Ozzie Albies became just the fourth middle infielder to hit 30 homers and 100 RBIs before age 22.

Albies wows Atlanta Braves fans with his exciting playing style at second base.

"Players from Curacao speak four different languages and grow up playing baseball," former Braves general manager John Coppolella said. "They have the intellect as well as the instincts."

Albies is no different. His instincts are evident in the field. Albies came through the Braves' system as a shortstop, only to move over to second base once he reached the major league level. He looks like he's been playing there his entire life.

"Good defender, always in the right place," former Braves outfielder Joey Terdoslavich said. "I don't know if it's just how they teach you in Curacao, but he's always in the right place at the right time."

That's no accident. When Albies was six years old, a friend asked him if he wanted to play baseball. The next day, Albies said, he was on the field. And he hasn't stopped playing since.

Albies's dedication to the game was obvious, even early in his career. With his three-run blast against the Los Angeles Dodgers in August 2017, Albies became the first major leaguer born in 1997 to hit a home run.

Albies said his entire life is based around family and baseball. Following his successful 2017 rookie season, Albies returned to Curacao. While there he went to work on swing adjustments suggested by his minor league coaches. He'd spend his evenings staring at phone videos of that day's workouts, pouring over footage of his swing.

CALLED SHOT

It's never too early to start calling your shots. Before heading to the plate in the 11th inning of a 4-4 game against the Cincinnati Reds in June 2018, Albies turned to teammate Danny Santana and said, "It's time to go long now." Then he went ahead and launched a home run off the first pitch. It was Albies's first walk-off homer.

"He's real into his game," Braves manager Brian Snitker said. "He's a very dedicated guy and focused."

That showed in an April 2018 Braves win over the Chicago Cubs. On one play, Albies ran over to the second base bag to cover a stolen base attempt. One problem—Cubs catcher Willson Contreras grounded the pitch to where Albies was originally standing. No matter. Albies simply sprinted all the way back to his original station, fielded the grounder, and threw Contreras out.

Later in the game, the Cubs' Kyle Schwarber hit a hard line drive. Albies ranged far into the hole and made a full-extension dive. Getting to the ball was impressive enough, but Albies quickly popped up and threw Schwarber out for good measure.

"He's an exciting player," Snitker said. "He's steady, and I'm not surprised by anything anymore. He's just a really good little player."

Albies's small frame suggested he wasn't going to be a power bat. His minor league stats supported that as well. Through his first three years of professional baseball, Albies hit a total of seven home runs. But things changed when he reached the major leagues. Albies recorded 22 extra base hits in the first month of the 2018 season. That was the most ever recorded by a Braves player before the end of April.

The power didn't let up. Albies hit 24 home runs and 72 RBIs on the season, giving him 30 and 100 for his career. Until that point, only three middle infielders had reached those milestones at age 21 or younger. And in doing so, he helped the Braves make a surprise run to the playoffs.

"I have every confidence, and I think everybody does, in him as a player," Snitker said.

OZZIE ALBIES AT-A-GLANCE

BIRTHPLACE: Willemstad, Curacao

BIRTH DATE: January 7, 1997

POSITION: Second base

BATS: Both

THROWS: Right

SIZE: 5'8", 165 pounds

TEAM: Atlanta Braves

MAJOR LEAGUE DEBUT: August 1, 2017 (vs. the Los Angeles Dodgers)

SIGNED AS AN INTERNATIONAL FREE AGENT BY THE BRAVES IN 2013

CHAPTER 3

MOOKIE BETTS

Don't let Mookie Betts's size fool you. Despite being one of the smallest players on the Boston Red Sox at 5-foot-9 and 180 pounds, Betts is one of the team's biggest sluggers. His stature may not intimidate you, but his bat sure will.

The Los Angeles Angels learned that the hard way in April 2018. Coming back from an injury scare, Betts led off for the Red Sox with a solo shot off ace pitcher Shohei Ohtani. In the third inning, he went yard again, this time off reliever Luke Bard. Then, in the eighth, Betts launched a three-run shot to left field off Cam Bedrosian. The Sox, unsurprisingly, won 10–1.

"Any time you can kind of do something like that, it's huge to help the team," Betts said afterward. "I just ride the wave."

Mookie Betts has become one of the most consistent power threats for the Boston Red Sox.

In fact, it was the third time Betts rode that wave by hitting three home runs in a game. Only two other players had matched that feat before turning 26 years old, and one was a Hall of Famer. Meanwhile, only one other Red Sox hitter had matched the feat. That player? Ted Williams, considered by many to be the best pure hitter in the history of baseball.

And Betts didn't share the record with the legendary Williams for long. In May, he had his fourth three-homer game to take the record all for himself.

That feat highlighted just how good Betts is at the plate, where he is one of the most dangerous leadoff hitters in the league. But what makes Betts so special is that he's also a great fielder, having won Gold Glove awards at a position he didn't grow up playing.

He is the ultimate five-tool player organizations dream about drafting.

Betts's full name is Markus Lynn Betts, making his initials M. L. B. Baseball might have been Betts's destiny, though his nickname was inspired by a basketball player: Mookie Blaylock. During his high school years in Tennessee, Betts starred mostly as an infielder. The Red Sox thought enough of the player to select him in the fifth round of the 2011 MLB draft.

Now a star in the majors, Betts credits basketball—a sport he also played through high school—for much of his success. It's the sport where he learned how to adjust. Betts recalled a specific game where an opponent blocked his shot multiple times. Eventually, he found a way to get his shot off. He takes the same approach to the baseball field.

"You have a 2-0 count and you think no way they'll throw a breaking ball, and they do it," Betts said. "Now my body naturally adjusts that maybe I can hit a 2-0 hanger. It's just kind of natural."

Betts doesn't watch a lot of film on pitchers. He doesn't overanalyze at-bats.

"I like that I can just naturally adjust," Betts said. "If I know a pitcher has this or that, I'm not going to change my plan on purpose. As the at-bat goes, I'm sure my body and my mind will adjust."

The communication he learned as a basketball point guard helped him transition on the baseball diamond. Betts played second base for most of his minor league career, but Dustin Pedroia was already entrenched in that position for the Red Sox. So Betts switched to the outfield, where communicating and calling balls is critical. In 2018, he won his third consecutive Gold Glove award as the best defensive right fielder in the American League (AL).

"He's the best right fielder I've ever seen in person," Baltimore Orioles manager Buck Showalter said. "The dynamic he creates for them defensively in right field at Fenway is a big advantage for Boston."

Betts is equally as entertaining on the base paths. Although he doesn't put up gaudy stolen base numbers—his career high in a season is 30 in 2018—he makes the types of plays that electrify fans. In a May 2018 game against the Texas Rangers, Betts scored from first on a bloop hit that flew all of 174 feet.

Betts's crossover ability even extends to bowling, ping-pong, and pool. Teammates say they can't beat him, due to Betts's awesome hand-eye coordination. Maybe that's why he's nearly impossible to strike out, too.

In April 2017, Toronto Blue Jays pitcher Francisco Liriano got Betts to swing and miss on a 2–2 slider for strike three. Why is that significant? It marked Betts's first strikeout in 129 regular-season plate appearances, marking the league's longest K-free stretch since 2004. In today's game, where strikeouts are shrugged off as a worthwhile trade-off in the pursuit of power, such a stretch is hard to fathom.

Credit those hands, those eyes, and that mind. Betts can solve a Rubik's Cube in approximately two minutes, so it shouldn't come as a surprise that he can recognize a pitch in a split second.

It's all contributed to Betts's early success. He had two All-Star Game appearances, won a Silver Slugger award, and twice finished in the top six in AL Most Valuable Player (MVP) voting results before turning 25 years old.

And he continues to improve.

Already a power threat through his first four major league seasons, Betts hit a career-high 32 home runs in 2018. The improvement was credited to an

TOP TALKER, TOO

Betts has a wide range of skills. Turns out, talking is one of them. In 2018, ESPN had Betts miked up for a spring training game against the Chicago Cubs. In the third inning, Betts was providing in-game commentary from right field. Then, while he was midsentence, Kris Bryant laced a ball into the right field corner. As Betts sprinted to chase down the liner, he told ESPN's commentators, "I ain't getting this one, boys." Betts did eventually track down the ball and throw it into the infield, but not before Bryant recorded a triple.

There were lots of smiles as Betts and the Red Sox won 108 games and then the World Series in 2018.

adjustment he made prior to the season. Betts used to rely mostly on his hands in his swing. In 2018, he started using the rest of his body.

"I am able to use the muscles I work out with," Betts said. "I thought it was hands that generated my power. It's not just that. I thought it was pretty much 'swing harder and you'll hit it further' and that is not necessarily the case. Use everything to swing."

In addition to his career high in home runs, Betts led the AL with a .346 batting average and 84 extra-base hits in 2018, while tying for the league lead in runs, even though he played in just 136 games. He also became only the 40th player ever to hit at least 30 homers and steal at least 30 bases in a season. The effort helped lead the Red Sox to the World Series, where they beat the Los Angeles Dodgers. A few days later, Betts was named the league's MVP. That Betts continues to find ways to improve from one year to the next is impressive, given his apparent lack of weaknesses.

MOOKIE BETTS AT-A-GLANCE

BIRTHPLACE: Nashville, Tennessee
BIRTH DATE: October 7, 1992
POSITION: Right fielder
BATS: Right
THROWS: Right
SIZE: 5'9", 180 pounds
TEAM: Boston Red Sox
MAJOR LEAGUE DEBUT: June 29, 2014 (vs. the New York Yankees)
DRAFTED BY THE RED SOX 172ND OVERALL IN 2011

CHAPTER 4

ALEX BREGMAN

Houston Astros third baseman Alex Bregman used baseball's biggest stage to showcase his wide set of skills. Competing against the Los Angeles Dodgers in the 2017 World Series, he showed off with the bat, with the glove, and with a clutch gene that continually shows up in the biggest of moments.

Game 5 against the Dodgers went to extra innings. The teams had split the first four games. Now they were tied 12–12 in the 10th inning. That's when Bregman stepped up to the plate. With two outs and runners on first and second, Bregman had a chance to push the series in Houston's favor.

"It's your time," Astros shortstop Carlos Correa told Bregman. The 6-foot Bregman dug into the batter's box, ready to face off against Dodgers' star closer

Alex Bregman's defense was a key part in the Houston Astros winning the 2017 World Series.

Kenley Jansen. Bregman planned on taking the first pitch of the at-bat, until he didn't. Instead, Bregman lined a single to left center, driving in Derek Fisher to give the Astros a 3–2 series lead.

"It makes everything worth it; every weight that you lifted in the offseason, every swing that you took in the cage," said Bregman, a native of Albuquerque, New Mexico. "When you feel like you came through for your team, and you see the joy on their faces, there's nothing like it. It's such a special feeling that I'm so fortunate and blessed to feel."

He better get used to it.

In fact, while many of his teammates took a step back in 2018, Bregman made notable improvements. He had career highs in batting average (.286), home runs (31), and RBIs (103), while adding a league-high 51 doubles. Then he batted .556 with two home runs in a playoff series against Cleveland, though the Astros fell short of reaching another World Series.

Bregman's future as a bright baseball prospect might have been sealed when as a four-year-old he recorded an unassisted triple play . . . in his first T-ball game. He was projected to be a first-round pick out of high school before he missed much of his senior campaign due to injury. While fielding pregame grounders, Bregman missed one and the ball shattered a knuckle on his right hand. The injury led to every team passing on Bregman in the first round of the 2012 draft. Eventually, the Boston Red Sox selected him in the 28th round, but Bregman elected to go to play college baseball for Louisiana State.

Bregman wore the No. 30 on his jersey as a freshman in college, a symbol of the 30 teams that passed on him on draft night. He spent the next three years with the Tigers reestablishing his draft stock. When he reentered the draft in 2015, the Astros picked him second overall. Now in Houston, he wears the No. 2 because "he knows he should have been the first pick, not the second, in the draft," Alex's father, Sam Bregman, said.

Maybe dad was right. Alex Bregman ripped up the minor leagues, earning USA *Today*'s Minor League Player of the Year award in 2016, the same season he made his Astros debut. Bregman's early major league days didn't go as well. He went hitless in his first 18 major league at-bats, starting his Astros career on a 1-for-34 streak.

"By my 10th at-bat I was getting booed," he joked.

Yet the Astros had no concern that Bregman's early failures would stunt his growth. Mike Elias, Houston's assistant general manager, said Bregman's makeup is what sold the Astros on the infielder.

"He exudes a confidence and a work ethic and a competitive focus that is special," Elias said. "If you watch him carefully, there's an aura about him when he's on the field that he's going to win the game come (heck) or high water."

He showed that in the 2017 playoffs. With Houston trailing Boston in the eighth inning of Game 4 in the AL Division Series (ALDS), Bregman hit a game-tying homer. Houston went on to clinch the series. In Game 7 of the AL Championship Series (ALCS), the Astros led the New York Yankees 1–0 in the fifth inning. On a soft chopper, Bregman charged the ball and delivered a strike to throw out a runner at home. And in Game 4 of the World Series, Bregman struck again. This time he made a similar play, charging in on a grounder, fielding it on a short hop, and then throwing out the runner to keep the game scoreless in the sixth inning.

"He is cool and calm and completely in control of himself in these moments," Astros manager A. J. Hinch said.

Bregman celebrates after hitting a game-winning single in Game 5 of the 2017 World Series.

A lifelong shortstop, Bregman's versatility made it possible for him to move over to third base in the majors. This allowed him to play next to Houston's star shortstop, Carlos Correa. The transition was a smooth one, as evidenced by a game against the Oakland Athletics in August 2017. Bregman recorded seven assists in eight innings at the hot corner. Then in back-to-back games in April 2018, Bregman ranged far to his right to field ground balls, planted his foot five feet into foul territory—near the third base coach's box—and gunned down runners at first.

"He's literally a shortstop playing third," Melvin said. "The (plays he makes) on the run, especially to his backhand, shortstops are used to making those plays."

Bregman is one of the primary reasons many consider Houston to possess the game's best defensive infield. In the field, Bregman has a strong arm and plenty of range. At the plate, he hits for power and rarely strikes out. In a Houston lineup crowded with stars, Bregman still manages to stand out.

"You're talking about a 23-year-old kid who plays like a 30-year-old veteran," Astros second baseman Jose Altuve, the 2017 AL MVP, said. "He hits homers, he

NO MO MUSTACHE

Bregman sported an impressive mustache as he stepped into the batter's box in the second inning of a game against the Kansas City Royals in June 2018. When he came back to the plate in the fourth inning, the mustache was gone. "I just shaved it," Bregman explained. The midgame facial hair transformation caused a stir on social media, but not so much in the Houston dugout. Astros manager A. J. Hinch said he didn't notice the change. Neither did most of his teammates.

steals bases. I remember when I was 23 and I wasn't as good as him, so I feel like he's going to be a superstar."

Yet despite all of Bregman's skills, it's his mentality and ability to come through when needed most that set him apart early in his career.

"He's not scared at all," Astros pitcher Justin Verlander said. "I think you can see in some of the defensive plays he's made and some of the home runs he's hit against the pitchers that he hit them against, he thrives in big moments. When the pressure is on, he's a guy you want in your corner."

ALEX BREGMAN AT-A-GLANCE

BIRTHPLACE: Albuquerque, New Mexico

BIRTH DATE: March 30, 1994

POSITION: Third baseman

BATS: Right

THROWS: Right

SIZE: 6', 180 pounds

TEAM: Houston Astros

MAJOR LEAGUE DEBUT: July 25, 2016 (vs. the New York Yankees)

DRAFTED SECOND OVERALL BY THE HOUSTON ASTROS IN 2015

CHAPTER 5

KRIS BRYANT

It took one throw across the diamond to fulfill Kris Bryant's legacy.

One out away from the Chicago Cubs' first World Series title in 108 years, it was only fitting the ball would find the man dubbed by many to be the franchise's "savior."

Cleveland's Michael Martinez hit a slow chopper to third. Bryant fielded the ball. As he fired it to first, his cleats gave out on the wet grass beneath him. No matter, Bryant's throw was a strike, easily in time to record the final out to end the Cubs' agonizing championship drought.

"I'm out here crying, man," Bryant said on the field after the game. "I am so happy. I can't even really put into words how this feels."

Kris Bryant celebrates as the Chicago Cubs clinch the World Series title in 2016.

Selected with the No. 2 pick in the 2013 draft, the 6-foot-5 third baseman came to Chicago with great potential. "He was supposed to be the savior of the city," Cubs pitcher Jon Lester said.

Bryant has not disappointed.

Good luck finding a trophy case capable of housing all of his hardware. Bryant won the Dick Howser Trophy—the honor given to the best college baseball player—in 2013 as a junior at San Diego. In 2014, Bryant was named the minor league player of the year by both USA *Today* and *Baseball America.* In 2015, he earned National League (NL) Rookie of the Year honors. Bryant was named NL MVP in 2016 while leading the Cubs to that previously elusive title. By the time he turned 26 years old, Bryant was already a two-time All-Star who'd finished in the top 11 of NL MVP voting three times.

So what is it exactly that makes Bryant so great? Look no further than Game 5 of the 2016 World Series.

Down three games to one, their backs were against the wall, and trailing 1–0 in the fourth inning, the Cubs needed a spark. That's when Bryant stepped into the batter's box. One swing later, the Cubs had new life. Bryant's blast to left center tied the game, perhaps providing the spark not only to Chicago's Game 5 comeback, but its rally to win the World Series.

"We're down in an elimination game, and he ties it up with one swing," Cubs first baseman Anthony Rizzo said. "We fed off it."

Bryant hit 94 homers over his first three major league seasons, thanks largely to his swing. A *Sports Illustrated* reporter analyzed Bryant's swing. He found that Bryant gets his bat into the hitting zone early, keeps his elbow back to create a shorter swing path, and rolls his back foot to keep his hip from firing too soon. First his front hip comes through, then his hands, followed by his back hip, which is all trailed by the bat head.

Former Cubs hitting coach John Mallee told *Sports Illustrated* Bryant "has the prototype of the modern swing."

Despite Bryant's natural ability, his pro career hasn't always been easy. In his debut with the Class-A Boise Hawks, Bryant struck out four times. Former Cubs special assistant Anthony Iapoce was at the game. Members of Chicago's front office were texting him to see what was going wrong.

After the fourth strikeout, Bryant walked by.

"Tough start!" Iapoce recalled Bryant saying with enthusiasm.

In his fifth at-bat, Bryant struck out again. Five Ks doesn't inspire confidence, but it didn't seem to affect Bryant, who went on to hit .354 that season in Boise.

"I don't think I ever saw KB panic," Iapoce said. "We got big guys in the minor leagues all over the place that stink with the same talent, but they don't know how to think it, the fear, the anxiety. Those guys like Kris, they're able to filter that stuff out and they still play like they're 12 years old. KB still plays like he's 12. (He never lost) that feeling when you walk out on the field: 'I'm the best player and we're going to win today.'"

LEARNING FROM THE BEST

Kris's father, Mike Bryant, is the scientist behind his son's swing. Mike learned from Hall of Famer Ted Williams, both through study of Williams's book, *The Science of Hitting*, and hands-on experience. As a minor leaguer, Mike Bryant took part in spring training workout sessions with Williams. The main points transferred from Williams's lessons to Kris Bryant's approach: swing at pitches you can drive, and swing upward to counter the pitcher's downward plane.

Bryant is capable of playing the corner infield spots and every outfield position. He'll always run out a ground ball with 100 percent effort and will take the extra base whenever possible. But it's his mentality that has given him the ability to become the player he is—the Chicago Cubs' savior.

"The sky's the limit," Cubs manager Joe Maddon said. "The guy's dedicated, motivated, athletic. He takes care of himself. Multiple positions, MVP winner who does not care where you put him in the lineup, whether it's offensively or defensively. He's kind of the manager's dream."

KRIS BRYANT AT-A-GLANCE

BIRTHPLACE: Las Vegas, Nevada
BIRTH DATE: January 4, 1992
POSITION: Third baseman
BATS: Right
THROWS: Right
SIZE: 6'5", 230 pounds
TEAM: Chicago Cubs
MAJOR LEAGUE DEBUT: April 17, 2015 (vs. the San Diego Padres)
DRAFTED SECOND OVERALL BY THE CHICAGO CUBS IN 2013

CHAPTER 6

CARLOS CORREA

With a World Series championship, an All-Star Game appearance, and the 2015 AL Rookie of the Year Award under his belt by the time he turned 23 years old, Carlos Correa set his career sights even higher prior to the 2018 season.

"MVP is something I don't want to retire without winning," the Houston Astros shortstop said. "At some point, I'd like to win that, and I'll just try to improve my game every single day to try to accomplish that."

"I don't want to be one of the top (players)," he added. "I want to be the top one."

He might be well on his way. The Astros picked Correa with the first pick in the 2012 draft. Ever since, the 6-foot-4 Puerto Rico native has been redefining the prototypical shortstop body while mashing at the

A strong work ethic has helped Carlos Correa become one of the Houston Astros' best young players.

plate. So if Correa plans to win MVP one day, history suggests that's what he will do.

"He can do anything in this game," Astros manager A. J. Hinch said. "He's one of the most talented and one of the most hard-working players in the big leagues."

At 6-foot-4, Cal Ripken Jr. was one of the original big-build shortstops during the 1980s and 1990s. The Hall of Famer marveled at the new generation of big shortstops, such as Correa, saying they possess "a unique set of physical skills."

"You're seeing bigger, more athletic players adapt that to a position that was thought of originally as one that a smaller person had to play," Ripken said.

WIN AND A WEDDING

In the moments following the Astros' 2017 World Series win, Carlos Correa took one more big swing. It was another home run. During a live postgame interview on Fox, Correa called winning the World Series "one of the biggest accomplishments of my life, and right now I want to take another big step in my life." He pulled out a ring, looked at his girlfriend and asked, "Daniella Rodriguez, will you make me the happiest man in the world? Will you marry me?" She said yes.

Correa is leading that charge. His defensive abilities were evident as a young player, Astros assistant general manager Mike Elias said. So even though Correa was big for baseball's most physically demanding infield position, the team saw a future for him as a shortstop.

"He's always been a very special defender," Elias said. "Perfect throwing motion, top of scale arm strength, and very slick hands. . . . When you added all of this together, despite being very big for the position, he had a good chance to stay at shortstop."

Still, after Correa was drafted, he recalled people continuing to predict that he would outgrow the position.

"I think I've proved them wrong," Correa said.

And he continues to do so with plays like the one he made against the New York Yankees in May 2018. Yankees second baseman Gleyber Torres hit a ball deep into the hole, forcing Correa to range far to his right. Correa traveled nearly 58 feet to track the grounder down, fielding it well into the outfield grass in left. While still on the run, Correa jumped up and fired to first. The one-hopper from 149 feet away was on the money to get Torres by a half step.

"It's one of the best plays I've ever seen made in person," Astros pitcher Lance McCullers Jr. said. "Just the way he made the play, the way he's been playing all year. He's special over there."

What makes Correa truly special, though, is that he's also a force at the plate. Elias said that Correa always had a "tremendous amount of raw power," and that the ball "jumped off his bat in a way that was very different from most kids in that draft."

Correa credits much of his success to his core strength, which comes from his abdominal and lower back muscles. During the offseason, he said he spends two hours at the gym every day.

"A lot of baseball moves come from your core," Correa said. "A strong core helps you to hit, play defense, dive for the ball, to throw, to do it all."

Correa also focuses on leg strength. "I use squats, split squats, hamstring workouts to build muscle and make sure my legs have the strength to stay healthy for all 162 games," he said.

The payoff for all that hard work shows up in big situations, such as when Correa hit five home runs in 18 playoff games during the Astros' run to the 2017 World Series title.

Correa rounds the bases after hitting a key home run in Game 5 of the 2017 World Series.

"THIS IS A GUY THAT WORKS RELENTLESSLY AND VERY SMARTLY AT HIS CRAFT AND HE'S IMPROVED HIS SWING."

—ASTROS ASSISTANT GENERAL MANAGER MIKE ELIAS

The power was somewhat expected out of Correa. Where the shortstop has "exceeded expectations," Elias said, is with how well he's hit for average. In 2017, Correa hit .315, well up from his .276 average over his first two major league seasons.

"This is a guy that works relentlessly and very smartly at his craft and he's improved his swing," Elias said. "He is not only one of the most dangerous hitters in the league with his power, he is one of the tougher outs, too."

Correa's insistence on improvement stems from his upbringing. When he was growing up, starting in elementary school, his father would bring him to the park for two hours every night to work on baseball drills. No parties, no nothing.

That dedication remains with the Astros. During his early major league years, Correa's daily schedule consisted of waking up, watching a TV show, going to the ballpark for 11 to 12 hours, and then coming home and going to bed. When not playing or working on his physical skills at the park, he could often be found studying his game. Correa uses a baseball bat sensor called Blast Motion to get data feedback on his swing and is consistently making minor adjustments.

"The trajectory he is on with natural improvements going into his prime years, I think you're going to see some amazing numbers," Elias said. "Knowing him and the way he works, he is not going to let any part of his game decline."

CARLOS CORREA AT-A-GLANCE

BIRTHPLACE: Ponce, Puerto Rico
BIRTH DATE: September 22, 1994
POSITION: Shortstop
BATS: Right
THROWS: Right
SIZE: 6'4", 215 pounds
TEAM: Houston Astros
MAJOR LEAGUE DEBUT: June 8, 2015 (vs. the Chicago White Sox)
DRAFTED FIRST OVERALL BY THE HOUSTON ASTROS IN 2012

CHAPTER 7

BRYCE HARPER

Many young athletes have been labeled a "prodigy" at a young age. Only a select few have gone on to fulfill that destiny. Bryce Harper was certainly one of them.

At age 16, Harper was featured on the *Sports Illustrated* cover. At 19 years old, he was the NL Rookie of the Year. And at 22 years old, he was the 2015 NL MVP—by unanimous vote. At every step, the Washington Nationals outfielder proved he was up to the challenge of living up to high expectations.

That shouldn't come as a surprise. Harper, a 6-foot-3 slugger, has always been a rarity.

Harper had a mythical-like status before ever joining a pro team. He was the kid who went 12-for-12 with 11 home runs at a traveling baseball tournament at age 13. He was the one who hit a home run his coaches

Before even putting on a Washington Nationals uniform, Bryce Harper was already a big-name talent.

measured out to 570 feet in high school. And it was Harper who hit a 502-foot home run at Tropicana Field, home of the Tampa Bay Rays, when he was 16 years old. That was the same age at which his fastball was clocked at 96 miles per hour.

So it was no wonder *Sports Illustrated* sent a writer to Harper's hometown of Las Vegas to profile the wonderboy at an age when most kids are just focused on getting their driver's licenses. And Harper wasn't just profiled. The popular magazine featured Harper on the cover, pushing NBA Finals coverage inside.

Next to a photo of Harper read the headline: "Baseball's Chosen One." A subtext declared Harper as "the most exciting prodigy since LeBron," as in basketball star LeBron James. How's that for something to live up to? But it didn't seem to bother Harper, who never backs away from the bright lights.

In the *Sports Illustrated* story, Harper listed his long-term goals as the following: "Be in the Hall of Fame, definitely. Play in Yankee Stadium. Play in the (Yankees') pinstripes. Be considered the greatest baseball player who ever lived. I can't wait."

Collecting six All-Star Game appearances in his first seven major league seasons, Harper is well on his way to a few of those feats.

He owes much of his success to his swing, a modern marvel that has drawn comparisons to that of legendary slugger Babe Ruth. Former Nationals hitting coach Rick Schu declared Harper's and Ruth's swings were "identical."

"They've got that exact same swing at contact point," Schu said.

A thorough *Washington Post* examination of Harper's swing revealed the slugger starts with his feet open and his hands behind his ear. He turns his neck more than most to get a good view of the pitcher with both eyes—including his dominant left eye—which allows him to see the ball and decipher the type of pitch earlier.

At the start of his swing, Harper puts his weight on his back leg, only to eventually plant his front leg and pick up his back foot as he twists his torso and transfers power to his upper body.

"His torque in his hips, all that stuff, everything is always together," former Nationals hitting coach Rick Eckstein said. "He utilizes his entire body to execute his swing. It's athleticism, strength, coordination—obviously, years of training."

Harper insists he never looked at anything mechanical with his swing. "The full thing is

God-given," he said. He just did what was comfortable, and he did it a lot—"millions" of reps worth of practice.

The result is a cut capable of producing jaw-dropping results. In June 2017, Harper legitimately tore the cover off a ball on a foul ball hit against Baltimore. About a week later, he hit a home run off New York Mets pitcher Robert Gsellman that left the park at 116.3 miles per hour.

"That was a different sound," Nationals pitcher Gio Gonzalez said. "He got it solid for sure. That ball left in a hurry. But then again, it's Bryce. Any time you hear a loud sound like that, you know it's going somewhere far and fast."

Nationals general manager Mike Rizzo compared Harper's combination of balance and bat speed to Tiger Woods swinging a golf club. Cincinnati Reds first baseman Joey Votto, also a past NL MVP winner, said most lefties have a sweeping swing path. Harper has "more of a flat, tomahawk, hammer path," Votto said, which produces more line drives.

Swing path and technique are nice, but brute force helps, too. In April 2018, Harper's bat snapped in half upon making contact in a game against the New York Mets. And yet the ball still traveled over the fence in

Harper's strength showed when he hit a broken-bat home run against the New York Mets in April 2018.

right-center field. Harper flexed his right biceps after he finished circling the bases.

"I said, 'Yeah, you're strong,'" Nationals manager Dave Martinez said.

That's the type of personality Harper tries to inject into baseball. Standing in the locker room after hitting a home run on Opening Day in 2016, Harper sported a hat that read "MAKE BASEBALL FUN AGAIN."

"Baseball's tired," Harper said. "It's a tired sport, because you can't express yourself. You can't do what people in other sports do. I'm not saying baseball is, you know, boring or anything like that . . ."

But he does think players should be able to show personality on and off the field, as is done in other sports, without the fear of catching a fastball to your ribs in your following at-bat.

> **"IF A GUY PUMPS HIS FIST AT ME ON THE MOUND, I'M GOING TO GO, 'YEAH, YOU GOT ME. GOOD FOR YOU. HOPEFULLY I GET YOU NEXT TIME.' THAT'S WHAT MAKES THE GAME FUN."**
>
> **–BRYCE HARPER**

"If a guy pumps his fist at me on the mound, I'm going to go, 'Yeah, you got me. Good for you. Hopefully I get you next time,'" Harper said. "That's what makes the game fun."

Harper is about the closest thing MLB has to an entertainer. He told ESPN about a situation in San Francisco during a playoff series against the Giants. Harper was in the on-deck circle when a fan who was holding a beverage started yelling at him.

"Hey, buddy," Harper said to the fan. "How's that glass of wine?"

The fan told Harper he was going to strike out.

"You know I love playing here, don't you, buddy?" Harper responded.

Harper proceeded to go up to the plate and hit a home run. Upon crossing home plate, Harper stared at the fan he had just exchanged words with.

Still, even Harper's showmanship has its limits. In 2015, Harper stopped taking pregame batting practice on the field in front of fans. The reason? It was too tempting to try to impress early-arriving fans, which increased the risk of developing bad habits.

"You don't want to be a 5 o'clock guy," he said, referring to the time of batting practice before a night game. "You want to be a 7:05 guy."

HEADED TO PHILLY

Harper and Manny Machado were the top prizes of the free agent class following the 2018 season. Machado ended up signing with the San Diego Padres, while Harper jumped to Philadelphia to play for the Nationals' NL East rival, the Phillies. On March 2, the Philadelphia Phillies introduced their new right fielder, who signed a 13-year, $330 million contract.

"I'm very happy and very proud to be able to put this uniform on and can't wait to do Phillie Nation proud," Harper said. "I'm excited to get started, and here's to a new chapter."

Harper put it all together that season, batting .330 with 42 home runs, while walking 124 times—all career highs. Twice in a three-week span Harper scored four runs in a game in which he didn't record a hit.

"He started grasping who Bryce Harper is," former Nationals shortstop Danny Espinosa said. "Rather than trying to create something more, to live up to someone else's idea of who he should be, he just grasped who Bryce was and ran with it."

At 22 years old, Harper became the third-youngest player to win the NL MVP Award. However, injures slowed his chances from repeating. In fact, Harper failed to play 120 games in three of his first six major league seasons.

It's a give and take with a player like Harper, who goes all-out on nearly every play. He's said he modeled his game after the likes of hustlers such as Pete Rose and Mickey Mantle. This can be seen every time he loses his helmet while sprinting around the bases or crashes into the outfield wall trying to catch a fly ball.

That type of effort and energy has helped make Harper one of the game's great players, but also consistently puts his body at risk. But don't expect Harper to change his ways.

Harper crashed into the wall at Dodger Stadium in Los Angeles in May 2013. The collision resulted in a laceration that required 11 stitches on his chin. No matter for Harper, who played two days later.

"I'm going to play this game for the rest of my life and try to play it as hard as I can every single day," Harper said. "My life being on the line, trying to kill myself out there for my team, trying to win a World Series, people can laugh at that all they want. At the end of the day, I'm going to look myself in the mirror and say I played this game as hard as I could."

BRYCE HARPER AT-A-GLANCE

BIRTHPLACE: Las Vegas, Nevada
BIRTH DATE: October 16, 1992
POSITION: Outfielder
BATS: Left
THROWS: Right
SIZE: 6'3", 220 pounds
TEAMS: Philadelphia Phillies (2019–), Washington Nationals (2012–18)
MAJOR LEAGUE DEBUT: April 28, 2012 (vs. the Los Angeles Dodgers)
DRAFTED FIRST OVERALL BY THE WASHINGTON NATIONALS IN 2010

CHAPTER 8

AARON JUDGE

Aaron Judge doesn't have authority to make a ruling in a courtroom. But he certainly knew how to make a statement in his major league debut. In his first at-bat, the New York Yankees' slugger blasted a 1–2 pitch 446 feet to center field.

Debuting with a home run always makes a nice impression. But Judge's longball off Tampa Bay Rays pitcher Matt Andriese was extra special. The August 2016 homer was just the third in history to bounce off or land over the glass panels above Monument Park in the new Yankee Stadium, which opened in 2009.

"There's not so many things you can say after something like that," former teammate Tyler Austin said. "That thing was hit a ton."

Aaron Judge wasted no time in proving to be the New York Yankees' next great power hitter.

And Judge's homer was just the first of many. He hit four in 27 games that season. And one year later, in 2017, the 25-year-old Judge hit 52 home runs. That broke the previous rookie record of 49 set by Mark McGwire in 1987. But Judge did so much more than that. In a team history flush with some of the game's great sluggers, Judge became just the fifth Yankee to hit 50 homers in a season. He also won that season's Home Run Derby and was named the AL Rookie of the Year. The only blemish was not winning the AL MVP Award. But he did finish second in the voting.

"It was an amazing, remarkable year that no one would have predicted," Yankees general manager Brian Cashman said.

The 2017 season was no fluke, though. In 2018, Judge reached 60 home runs in just 197 career games, faster than any player in history. Then he became the fastest to hit 70 homers (231 games).

But don't expect to see Judge buying into the hype. He is as humble as he is big and strong. He doesn't boast or celebrate after hitting a home run. He just puts his head down and rounds the bases. And when it was time to take the field again after his historic home run, Judge trotted back out to right field with

Judge watches as his 50th home run clears the fence in 2017, breaking Mark McGwire's long-standing rookie record.

an extra glove and hat for teammate Greg Bird, who had been stranded on the base paths.

"You have a special kid," former Yankees manager Joe Girardi said. "He's a natural-born leader. It's almost like he's a big brother. He watches out for everyone. You got the whole package."

Standing at 6-foot-7 and 282 pounds, Judge looks more like an offensive tackle than an outfielder. In fact, the Linden, California, native actually received more recruiting interest from collegiate football programs than baseball teams.

A star wide receiver in high school, Judge had scholarship offers from powerhouse programs such as Notre Dame, Stanford, and UCLA. His high school football coach thought Judge could've been a great defensive end. But Judge chose baseball, attending Fresno State on a partial scholarship.

"I fell in love with baseball at an early age," Judge said. "If I had to choose one, it was always going to be baseball."

To say Judge is a "big" baseball player is an understatement. Only two major leaguers ever have been both taller and heavier than Judge. And both of

JUDGE'S CHAMBERS

A special section was created at Yankee Stadium in 2017: The Judge's Chambers. Made to resemble a jury's box, the Yankees boxed off three rows in right field, near where Judge plays defense, for selected fans to sit each game. Fans sitting in the seats received Yankees robes and foam gavels, just like a judge. "It's pretty cool," Judge said. "When you come to a game, it's supposed to be fun for the players and the fans. I feel like it might be something that's fun for the fans out there." The chambers gained a little extra legitimacy in August 2017, when Supreme Court Justice Sonia Sotomayor, a lifelong Yankees fan, took her seat in the special section to watch a game.

them—Jon Rauch and Jeff Niemann—were pitchers. Among position players, only 12 players 6-foot-6 or taller had logged 1,000-plus major league at-bats through the 2017 season.

Being big in baseball causes some challenges. Some heftier players take positions where they don't have to move much, such as first base or designated hitter. That's not Judge's style. He's actually a good outfielder, often looking like a receiver as he tracks down fly balls.

However, tall players also have to navigate a larger strike zone. And strikeouts are far and away Judge's biggest wart. He struck out in half of his 84 major league at-bats in 2016, putting his 2017 roster spot in jeopardy. Judge had to earn his position in spring training, edging out Aaron Hicks for the last outfield spot late in camp.

During his otherwise remarkable 2017 season, Judge recorded at least one strikeout in 37 straight games, a major league record. In the 2017 playoffs, in which the Yankees reached the ALCS, Judge struck out 27 times in 13 games, setting a new postseason record (that was broken shortly thereafter). Judge struck out eight times in one day in a doubleheader against the Detroit Tigers in June of 2018. That, too, is a record.

The strikeouts can be challenging to deal with, but Judge tries not to dwell on the negative. After his eight-strikeout doubleheader—a "terrible day," as he called it—he said "the beauty of baseball is that I get to wake up to fresh, new at-bats tomorrow."

And the next day, he's often better.

"I saw frustration, but I didn't see him getting down, I never saw him stop working, I never saw him not believe in himself," Girardi said.

If anything, Judge's failures are his motivation. In the middle of his remarkable 2017 campaign, Judge revealed that he kept a note in his phone that read ".179." It was a reminder of his batting average during the 27 major league games he played in 2016.

"It's motivation to tell you don't take anything for granted," Judge said. "This game will humble you in a heartbeat. So I just try to keep going out there and play my best game every day, because I could hit .179 in a couple weeks."

In modern baseball, teams are also more willing to accept strikeouts in exchange for power, a trade-off that perfectly fits Judge's game. Though he strikes out a lot, he also offers absurd power. MLB's Statcast tracks exit velocity—the speed in which balls travel off the bat. In 2017, Judge recorded seven of the 12 hardest hits, routinely crushing balls at 118-plus miles per hour. One of his home runs dented a door in the Yankees' bullpen.

Judge's most impressive blast is a 495-foot bomb against Baltimore in June 2017. The ball sailed all the way over the Yankee Stadium bleachers. It was the farthest hit ball in the major leagues all season.

"He's scary, man," retired Boston Red Sox slugger David Ortiz said. "That's the scariest thing I've ever seen. A guy that big that hits like that, that's special."

AARON JUDGE AT-A-GLANCE

BIRTHPLACE: Linden, California

BIRTH DATE: April 26, 1992

POSITION: Right fielder

BATS: Right

THROWS: Right

SIZE: 6'7", 282 pounds

TEAM: New York Yankees

MAJOR LEAGUE DEBUT: August 13, 2016 (vs. the Tampa Bay Rays)

DRAFTED 32ND OVERALL BY THE NEW YORK YANKEES IN 2013

CHAPTER 9

FRANCISCO LINDOR

Francisco Lindor is a lot of things. The Cleveland Indians shortstop is an All-Star, the 2015 AL Rookie of the Year runner-up, and the winner of Silver Slugger and Gold Glove awards.

One thing Lindor is not? A power hitter.

At least that's what he'd tell you. The numbers, though, suggest otherwise.

Lindor belted a pair of doubles and a pair of home runs in a win over the Minnesota Twins in May 2018. It was the second time he'd done so that season, making him the fourth major leaguer since 1908 to have two such games in the same season. The two home runs were his ninth and 10th of May. This all after the 5-foot-11, switch-hitting leadoff man hit 33 home runs in 2017. But a power hitter? No, not Lindor.

Francisco Lindor produces for Cleveland with a combination of short singles and long home runs.

"When I hit 50 (home runs)," Lindor said. "Then you can call me a power hitter, but it won't happen."

Though Lindor improved upon his home run numbers again in 2018, he has a way to go to reach 50. But it can't be ruled out, especially given how good he is at just about everything else.

Upon entering the majors, Lindor was known primarily for his defense. With his range, mechanics, and strong arm, the Caguas, Puerto Rico, native was like a vacuum at short.

"His quick feet, decision-making, arm strength, quick hands, his knowledge of the game—all that allows him to lead the infield as a shortstop and be that field general," Indians assistant general manager Carter Hawkins said.

Those qualities are frequently on display. On Opening Day in 2018, Lindor robbed Seattle Mariners catcher Mike Marjama of a hit. Lindor made a full extension dive to knock down a ball heading up the middle that would've scored a runner from second base. Then he picked the ball up and threw Marjama out at first base.

"We're used to that kind of thing by now," Indians pitcher Corey Kluber said. "Take it for granted almost."

Lindor is the total package on defense, which helped him earn a Gold Glove at shortstop.

It's what Lindor has done since entering the big leagues in 2015. He won a Gold Glove at shortstop in 2016 and was one of three finalists to receive the honor again in 2017.

To thrive in the field, Lindor follows a few basic principles. For example, he makes sure to get

69

momentum behind every throw. He maintains a stiff wrist on flips to second. He works off his left leg so he is always in position to at least block a ball if it takes a nasty hop. And he consistently stays low.

Lindor maintains those principles by using a flat, pancake-like glove in spring training. It forces him to keep his feet moving and his eye on the ball.

But his knack for the spectacular was born out of time on a hill with his father. Lindor's father, Miguel, would fire yellow rubber balls skipping down a hill at

MR. SMILE

Just about every one of Lindor's highlight-reel-worthy efforts are followed by a wide grin. So it's fitting Lindor carries the nickname "Mr. Smile," for the joy with which he plays the game. Lindor literally smiled as he stood in the batter's box against Baltimore Orioles pitcher Jeremy Hellickson in September 2017, and he held the smile all the way through his swing as he hit a home run.

"I've just never been a fan of a guy that makes a great play and acts like he's done it 10,000 times," Lindor said. "Smile, man. That's what we play for. We've got to enjoy the game. Smiling doesn't mean you're hot-dogging it or disrespecting the game. It's a smile."

his son. Francisco had two options: stop the ball, or go chase it into the thicket.

"They'd skip pretty fast," Lindor said. "I just had to attack the ball and get that good hop. Once it went up, I'd charge the ball and try to get it before it bounces."

At times, Miguel would tell his son to "try to do something nice."

"I was always taught that making plays was pretty cool," Lindor said. "(My dad) would make me catch a lot of ground balls, and he always made it fun. It was never right at me. It was to the side. He let me have fun with it. He'd let me do tricks."

Lindor still does those tricks, only now on a slightly bigger stage. In June 2016, Kansas City

> "I WAS ALWAYS TAUGHT THAT MAKING PLAYS WAS PRETTY COOL. (MY DAD) WOULD MAKE ME CATCH A LOT OF GROUND BALLS, AND HE ALWAYS MADE IT FUN. IT WAS NEVER RIGHT AT ME. IT WAS TO THE SIDE. HE LET ME HAVE FUN WITH IT. HE'D LET ME DO TRICKS."
>
> —FRANCISCO LINDOR

Royals hitter Kendrys Morales hit a ball sharply up the middle. A shifted defense had Lindor playing on the second-base side. He dove to his right to field the screamer. But instead of rising up and throwing to first, Lindor flipped the ball to third baseman Jose Ramirez, who was lined up near the standard shortstop position. Ramirez threw Morales out at first.

"Tonight, he surprised us again," Indians pitcher Josh Tomlin said. "You never know what he's going to pull off. He's a special player. I'll keep saying it. He's fun to watch—that's for sure."

Nothing about Lindor's game is as surprising as his power. Former Indians teammate Giovanny Urshela said he never thought Lindor would be able to hit "20-some" homers in a season. Urshela isn't alone. That wasn't supposed to be Lindor's game. His power didn't come from hours spent bulking up in the gym, but from a refined understanding of which pitches he can drive. He learned this from experience and countless conversations with coaches and teammates.

> "YOU NEVER KNOW WHAT HE'S GOING TO PULL OFF. HE'S A SPECIAL PLAYER."
>
> –INDIANS PITCHER JOSH TOMLIN

"The more you play, the more teammates you talk to, the more coaches you talk to, the more pitches you see, you learn and get better," Lindor said. "And if you don't, then that's on you."

But even as the home runs pile up, Lindor maintains his commitment to staying aggressive on the base paths and laying down bunts when the opportunity presents himself.

"That's just me," Lindor said. "I'm not a power hitter."

Well, he is, but maybe it's best for his game if he doesn't know it.

"I try to stay within myself, get a good pitch and drive it," Lindor said. "If it goes out, it goes out. And if it doesn't go out and it goes as a hit, I'm good."

FRANCISCO LINDOR AT-A-GLANCE

BIRTHPLACE: Caguas, Puerto Rico

BIRTH DATE: November 14, 1993

POSITION: Shortstop

BATS: Both

THROWS: Right

SIZE: 5'11", 190 pounds

TEAM: Cleveland Indians

MAJOR LEAGUE DEBUT: June 14, 2015 (vs. the Detroit Tigers)

DRAFTED EIGHTH OVERALL BY THE CLEVELAND INDIANS IN 2011

CHAPTER 10

MANNY MACHADO

Manny Machado plays with "a swag."

That's how Baltimore Orioles outfielder Adam Jones put it. And Jones knows where his former teammate got it from.

"You look at him," Jones said, "you know he's a Miami guy."

Watch Machado play, and you know he's also one of baseball's best players.

The 6-foot-3 infielder out of Hialeah, Florida, plays with an infectious joy and attractive flair not often seen in previous generations. It's a style that fits in well with the Miami area, which is known for its high-energy yet easy-going style.

"He plays with an ease that will make people jealous," Jones said. "When he's making plays, it looks

Manny Machado isn't afraid to have some fun on the baseball diamond.

carefree. When he makes an error, if someone sees that same carefree attitude, they'll think he's not caring. But just 10 minutes before, they saw a play that nobody has made in a long time. Some guys just have to work harder for the simpler things, but not him."

Anytime fans show up to a game with Machado, there's a chance to see him do something spectacular. There's a reason he was selected to four All-Star games over his first seven major league seasons, all with the Orioles. And there's a reason that the Los Angeles Dodgers quickly pounced when the struggling Orioles made Machado available for a trade in 2018.

Machado is a beast with the bat. He hit 33-plus home runs in four consecutive seasons from 2015 to 2018. Orioles hitting coach Scott Coolbaugh told *Sports Illustrated* that Machado is "one of the special breeds" with his ability at the plate.

Still, most of the oohs and ahhs he induces are a result of his play in the field.

One of his more memorable robberies came in the 2017 World Baseball Classic. Playing for the Dominican Republic, Machado was at third base in a game against Venezuela. That's when slugger Miguel Cabrera hit a sharp grounder down the line.

It looked like a certain extra-base hit. Instead, Machado somehow got to it. He extended his glove past the foul line to nab the ball. Drifting well into foul territory, he then fired 158 feet across the diamond to first for the out.

His countless web gems in that World Baseball Classic earned Machado the nickname "el ministro de la defensa"–or the minister of defense.

"That boy, he's not human," Dominican Republic left fielder Gregory Polanco said. "He's from another planet. He's a great guy, he never gives up, and it's great to watch him play."

It's the type of play Orioles fans saw for years, but they had to wait until the 2018 season to see Machado play full time at his natural position: shortstop.

Baltimore selected Machado with the third pick in the 2010 draft with designs on him playing short. That's where Machado played in the minors. But by the time he was ready to break into the majors in 2012, Baltimore had a gaping hole at third base.

So the Orioles tried to quickly school Machado on playing the hot corner. Two weeks later, he was their best option at third. No experience at the defensive position? No matter. In 2013, Machado's first full major

Whether he's playing at shortstop or third base, Machado is capable of making big plays in the field.

league campaign and first full season at third base, he won a Gold Glove. Two years later, he won another.

"Whoever taught him to field a ground ball—kudos to him," Jones said. "Come teach my kids."

The key was early repetition. By the time Machado was nine years old, he and his uncle Gio would go to the field each night, where Gio would hit "bullets" at the youngster.

"That's how you get better," Machado said. "Don't let the ball hit you. Catch it or get out of the way. And if you get out of the way, that's when you have to stop playing. So you've got to stay in there."

Machado prefers working on his defense to batting. In his mind, defense is what wins games. Orioles manager Buck Showalter said that's where Machado differs from the game's other top players, most of whom are known primarily for their hitting.

"The separator for me is the impact the player has on both sides of the ball. There, Manny is as good as anyone in the game. He impacts us and our pitching staff nightly, whether he's hitting or not," Showalter said.

FanGraphs tracks advanced defensive stats. Among third basemen, it found Machado ranked

> "THAT'S HOW YOU GET BETTER. DON'T LET THE BALL HIT YOU. CATCH IT OR GET OUT OF THE WAY. AND IF YOU GET OUT OF THE WAY, THAT'S WHEN YOU HAVE TO STOP PLAYING. SO YOU'VE GOT TO STAY IN THERE."
>
> —MANNY MACHADO

among the top seven in defensive runs saved in four of his first five major league seasons. The one year he didn't was 2014. That year he played just 82 games due to multiple knee injuries.

"We're just trying to figure out a way to throw a pitch where they hit it toward Manny," Showalter said.

Part of the solution there might have been moving Machado back to shortstop in 2018. The re-acclimation process didn't take long. In an April game against the

PUBLIC ENEMY

Machado entered a four-game series in Boston in May 2017 as public enemy No. 1. Less than two weeks earlier, Machado's spikes had caught Red Sox second baseman Dustin Pedroia's leg. Machado was booed in Boston. Red Sox pitchers threw inside to him. But he never lost his focus. In one instance, Red Sox pitcher Chris Sale threw behind Machado's legs. A few innings later Machado took Sale deep, one of three home runs he hit during the four-game series.

"He handled it properly. He went deep later, and showed his way of retaliation," Orioles teammate Adam Jones said. "At the end of the day, the best way to speak in this game is with your bat, your glove, and not with your mouth, and he did a great job."

Toronto Blue Jays, Machado ranged deep to his right to field a grounder off the bat of Justin Smoak. He then threw across his body from shallow left field to record the out.

"You know the saying 'Don't try this at home'?" Showalter said. "That's Manny. What he does on the field, don't try that at home."

In 2019, Machado found a new home for himself. He stayed in Southern California, signing a 10-year, $300 million contract with the San Diego Padres.

MANNY MACHADO AT-A-GLANCE

BIRTHPLACE: Hialeah, Florida
BIRTH DATE: July 6, 1992
POSITION: Shortstop
BATS: Right
THROWS: Right
SIZE: 6'3", 185 pounds
TEAMS: San Diego Padres (2019–), Los Angeles Dodgers (2018), Baltimore Orioles (2012–2018)
MAJOR LEAGUE DEBUT: August 9, 2012 (vs. the Kansas City Royals)
DRAFTED THIRD OVERALL BY THE BALTIMORE ORIOLES IN 2010

CHAPTER 11

SHOHEI OHTANI

In baseball lore, there will never be a player quite like Babe Ruth. Shohei Ohtani could very well be like Ruth in at least in one respect, though. Not since Ruth played in the late 1910s had a player starred as both a regular pitcher and hitter in the major leagues.

Ohtani is attempting to change that.

The Japanese superstar signed with the Los Angeles Angels ahead of the 2018 season. He had thrived as both a hitter and a pitcher in his native Japan. In California, he planned to serve as the team's starting pitcher on some days and the designated hitter on others. It's an unthinkable feat in today's game, but it's one Ohtani is used to.

"Hitting and pitching, it's the only baseball I know," Ohtani said. "Doing only one and not the other doesn't

Shohei Ohtani shined as a hitter and pitcher during his 2018 rookie season with the Los Angeles Angels.

feel natural to me. I suppose it's an accomplishment—I'm doing what others are not. But, to me, this is just normal."

That's a main reason why Ohtani decided to start his pro baseball career in Japan. He thrived in both settings out of high school. But major league teams were interested in having him pitch or hit, not do both. So Ohtani joined the Hokkaido Nippon-Ham Fighters in Japan's top league. The team allowed the 6-foot-4 phenom to pitch and hit. And he did both well. In 2016, Ohtani hit .322 with 22 home runs and 54 walks in just 104 games at the plate. Meanwhile, he went 10–4 on the mound with a 1.86 earned-run average, striking out 174 batters in 140 innings.

"I haven't been scouting long enough to say a guy's a once-in-a-lifetime type of talent—but he's up there," former Cleveland Indians scout Dave DeFreitas said. "You don't see this level of athleticism, work ethic, and aptitude come along often."

Pulling double duty just isn't done in the majors. It's hard enough to be effective at hitting or pitching. Maintaining some level of success at each? That's downright impossible, baseball experts agreed. Even

Ruth stopped pitching to focus on hitting and fielding when he joined the New York Yankees in 1920.

If anyone has what it takes to pull it off, it could be Ohtani.

He made his first start for the Angels in April 2018. And he picked up his first win that day against the Oakland Athletics. His second start as a pitcher came a week later, also against Oakland. This time he went seven innings, allowing just one hit while striking out 12. Now he had two wins in two starts.

"That's as good a game as you can see pitched," Angels manager Mike Scioscia said.

In those first two starts, Ohtani threw 183 pitches. Of those, 56 were splitters. That's a high percentage of splitters. The pitch is difficult to throw. It looks like a fastball but is slower and drops sharply as it nears home plate. Ohtani's delivery and arm angle were especially effective. Hitters couldn't tell whether he was preparing to throw a 100-mph fastball or a 90-mph splitter. So of those 56 splitters, the A's put just six into play. None resulted in hits.

"(It) looks like a strike I feel like almost every time, but it never is," Angels infielder Zack Cozart said. "It

Ohtani lived up to high expectations when he shut down the Oakland Athletics in his first two starts.

just drops below the zone. That's how it comes out, the same as his fastball. It makes it tough as a hitter."

If those two starts alone made up Ohtani's MLB debut, that'd be impressive enough. But all the while, he was also showcasing his power from the plate. It took Ohtani all of two starts in the Angels' batting order to hit his first major league home run. It was a three-run blast off a curveball from Cleveland Indians starter Josh Tomlin. In his next game, Ohtani homered off Cleveland ace Corey Kluber. And in the game after that, Ohtani struck again, hitting a 449-foot bomb to center field off Oakland starter Daniel Gossett. Three games, three homers.

"It's getting old," shortstop Andrelton Simmons joked. "No, but it's really cool to see him swing the bat that well. I'm happy for him. I think we all are. He has big power, and he's showing it."

Power was nothing new for Ohtani. This is the same guy who literally hit a ball into the roof of the Tokyo Dome in a 2016 game. Had the ball not left the facility, it would have traveled an estimated

ONE OF THE GUYS

Some superstars demand special treatment. Ohtani isn't one of them. When Ohtani hit his first major league home run in April 2018, his teammates followed tradition by essentially giving Ohtani the silent treatment. Upon returning to the dugout, Ohtani proceeded to high-five a line of invisible people before going over to give teammate Ian Kinsler a hug. That's when his teammates finally caved and came over to celebrate Ohtani's achievement. Ohtani then reemerged from the Angels' dugout to give a curtain call to the home fans.

525 feet. But a change during spring training in 2018 turbocharged his already awesome power.

Angels hitting coach Eric Hinske suggested Ohtani abandon the leg kick load-up on his swing. Hinske said that would help Ohtani keep his head still, staying closer to the ground and behind the ball. Ohtani tested the advice in a batting practice session.

"He took BP and was hitting tanks (homers) everywhere," Hinske said. "He was like, 'That works. I'm in.' That was it."

Ohtani's natural talent is obvious. What makes everything come together, though, is his passion for the game. "He just absorbs baseball," Angels pitching coach Charles Nagy said. "He can't get enough of it."

Although injuries limited Ohtani's first MLB season, and Tommy John surgery took him off the mound for a while afterward, he still ended the 2018 season as the AL Rookie of the Year. So it's no surprise that the Angels still have high hopes for the player. His work ethic is a big reason why. Staffers load videos onto an iPad for Ohtani to take home and study at night. He's always looking at one aspect of the game or another. Angels general manager Billy Eppler said Ohtani approaches film study like a quarterback.

Cubs general manager Jed Hoyer, in scouting Ohtani, determined the player was "a baseball junkie."

Ohtani has to be. Remember, he has to know opposing pitchers and hitters. Having to pay that much attention to that many details would tax any pro athlete. But if anyone can handle it, it might be Ohtani.

"To want to be great along with the physical talent and mental side of it?" Hinske said. "We're part of something special here."

SHOHEI OHTANI AT-A-GLANCE

BIRTHPLACE: Oshu, Japan
BIRTH DATE: July 5, 1994
POSITION: Pitcher and designated hitter
BATS: Left
THROWS: Right
SIZE: 6'4", 203 pounds
TEAM: Los Angeles Angels
MAJOR LEAGUE DEBUT: March 29, 2018 (vs. the Oakland Athletics)
SIGNED AS AN INTERNATIONAL FREE AGENT WITH THE LOS ANGELES ANGELS IN 2017

CHAPTER 12

JOSE RAMIREZ

The strut tells you all you need to know about Jose Ramirez. What the 5-foot-9, 165-pound Swiss army knife lacks in size, he makes up for in swagger. Confidence is one of baseball's most precious assets, and few possess as much of it as the Cleveland Indians' third baseman.

"That's just what I'm like," Ramirez, a Dominican Republic native, said. "I've always had confidence in myself. I don't worry about anything. I'm the same always."

That helps explain how Ramirez went from a can't-find prospect to a major league All-Star.

His teammates see that confidence every day, before Ramirez even takes the field. It's evident when he strolls into the locker room. Ramirez has earned

Jose Ramirez is a confident player who consistently produces at the plate for the Cleveland Indians.

the nickname George Jefferson, an ode to the popular 1970s sitcom character. Teammates say Ramirez's gait mimics Jefferson's striking strut. Ramirez strolls around with his chest puffed as he sways side to side with his waddle-like walk.

"It's the outside heel to inside toe. I think that's the key," former Indians catcher Chris Gimenez said.

Indians second baseball Jason Kipnis said Ramirez has "kind of got that little-man syndrome mixed with a confidence about him."

The former is easily explained. As a baseball player growing up in a baseball-rich country, nothing

JOSE AT YOUR GROCERY STORE

Ramirez is a brand name, and not just in baseball. The Cleveland Coffee Company named a coffee after him. Titled "Jose! Jose!," the packaging even pictured Ramirez's face. A percentage of the coffee sales were donated to the Cleveland Boys & Girls Club. When Ramirez made the All-Star team in 2017, he celebrated by purchasing 500 bags of the coffee and handing them out to fans. And, in 2018, Ramirez launched his "Jose Jose salsa." It hit the shelves of grocery stores in northeast and central Ohio. Proceeds from sales benefit Cleveland Indians Charities.

about Ramirez stuck out. His game never screamed "can't-miss prospect." Growing up, he didn't throw the ball that hard, hit it that far, or run that fast.

"He wasn't like a lot of the players down there who are long and lean and underdeveloped," John Mirabelli, the Indians' senior director of scouting operations, said. "He wasn't really sexy in scouting terms, so he flew way under the radar."

The measurables weren't there, but Ramirez's production was. The box score stats were always impressive. Still, Cleveland was the only team to offer Ramirez a contract. And even that was for a paltry $50,000.

After signing in 2009, Ramirez bounced around the organization. It wasn't until 2016 that he stuck around in the big leagues, and that was largely thanks to his versatility.

An infielder by trade, Ramirez found himself pushed into the starting left field spot when a teammate was injured in early 2016. Ramirez had played left field just three times in the minor leagues. No matter, he proved capable of catching fly balls. Soon it became clear that there's no position on the diamond that he

Ramirez throws off one leg to nail a base runner during a 2018 game.

can't defend. He started games at second, third, short, and left field in both 2015 and 2016.

The versatility extends to the batting order. Ramirez batted in all nine spots in the Indians' order in 2016. And he hit that milestone less than halfway

through the season. Indians manager Terry Francona said that Ramirez's versatility is more important to Cleveland than his production. Teammates agreed.

"Regardless of where you put him, he's going to get the job done," said shortstop Francisco Lindor.

And he'll do it well. Ramirez hit .312 in 2016. Then he followed that up by hitting .318 with 29 home runs and an AL-best 56 doubles. That was good enough for an All-Star Game berth, a Silver Slugger award, and a third-place finish in the AL MVP race. One year later, in 2018, he made a second All-Star Game and surpassed 100 RBIs for the first time.

Once a little-known prospect, Ramirez has become a bona fide star. These days, fans and teammates can't get enough of him.

"He doesn't strike out, he hits homers, he hits for average, he hits doubles, he runs, he steals, plays great defense," pitcher Trevor Bauer said. "The guy's a great baseball player."

In June 2017, Ramirez became the first player in the modern era to compile 14 extra-base hits in a seven game span. In an early September matchup against the Detroit Tigers, he tied a major league record with five extra-base knocks—three doubles and two home runs.

Indians hitting coach Ty Van Burkleo described Ramirez's plate approach as "very aggressive and very fearless." You're not going to find Ramirez playing tentatively on the diamond.

"The kid just has no fear," Mirabelli said. "He's always been confident. He's always played with an edge. He had a high motor, even back then (in Venezuela). He probably needed that mind set because everyone overlooked him."

It's impossible to overlook Ramirez now. He walks too tall.

"Coolest little guy on the planet," Indians outfielder Rajai Davis said. "When you hold your head up high like that, you walk with confidence, he's letting everybody know, 'I'm the most confident man on the field.'"

JOSE RAMIREZ AT-A-GLANCE

BIRTHPLACE: Bani, Dominican Republic

BIRTH DATE: September 17, 1992

POSITION: Third base

BATS: Both

THROWS: Right

SIZE: 5'9", 165 pounds

TEAM: Cleveland Indians

MAJOR LEAGUE DEBUT: September 1, 2013 (vs. the Detroit Tigers)

SIGNED AS AN INTERNATIONAL FREE AGENT BY THE INDIANS IN 2009

CHAPTER 13

GARY SANCHEZ

Gary Sanchez has plenty of power, in both his arm and his bat.

The latter showed in August 2017. The 6-foot-2, 230-pound catcher turned on a high changeup from Detroit Tigers pitcher Matthew Boyd, sending the pitch 493 feet to left field.

"When I hit that ball, I knew I hit it hard," Sanchez said through a translator. "But I had no clue it went that far—493 feet is very far."

It was the second longest home run hit in 2017. And if that wasn't enough, the Dominican Republic native hit a second home run later in the game. That's not something catchers often do.

Gary Sanchez's home run against the Detroit Tigers in August 2017 went an amazing 493 feet.

"He's very strong, he's got great bat speed, he's got the ability to adjust to pitches," said former Yankees manager Joe Girardi. "Let's not forget what he's done."

As a rookie in 2016, Sanchez hit 20 home runs in just 53 games. That's a pace of 61 home runs in a 162-game season.

"And it's not like he's just getting them out," former Yankees first baseman Mark Teixeira said. "He's hitting home runs 450 feet. He's crushing balls. . . . This guy is just squaring up balls like I don't think I've ever seen,"

THE KRAKEN

Prior to the 2016 season, Yankees general manager Brian Cashman said he'd like to "unleash the Kraken" in the coming season. But he wasn't referring to the sea monsters in the movie *Clash of the Titans*. He was referring to his top young catcher, Sanchez. The nickname stuck. When Sanchez got rolling following an injury-plagued start to 2017, Cashman declared, "The Kraken is back." Sanchez has embraced the nickname, even using Kraken-themed bats during the 2017 Home Run Derby. "I like the Kraken," Sanchez said. "I like anything the fans want to call me, as long as it's said in a positive light."

That stretch powered Sanchez to a second-place finish in the AL Rookie of the Year race, despite playing just a third of a major league season. He finished behind only Detroit Tigers pitcher Michael Fulmer.

Sanchez followed that up by hitting 33 home runs in his second season, despite missing 20 games early in the campaign due to a bicep strain. That total marked the most homers by a catcher in Yankees history. Two Yankees legends, Yogi Berra and Jorge Posada, had each hit 30.

For all of Sanchez's success at the plate, however, his defense behind the plate remains a work in progress. Sanchez committed a host of mistakes in a loss to the Cleveland Indians in August 2017. He was slow to apply a tag on a play at the plate. He allowed a passed ball. He made a poor throw on an attempt to throw out a runner stealing second. He couldn't keep a pair of wild pitches in front of him. And this was all in one game.

"He needs to improve, bottom line," Girardi said after the game. For the season, Sanchez led the AL with 16 passed balls in 2017.

Luckily for the Yankees, Sanchez's arm makes up for some of his fielding blunders. His first major

Sanchez has shown the ability to improve and make plays from behind the plate.

league start as a catcher came in August 2016 against Cleveland. In that game, Sanchez threw out two potential base stealers.

In 2017, Sanchez's average throws to throw out base runners were clocked at a major league best 87.8 miles per hour. The time between the ball hitting his glove to it hitting the infielder's glove on an attempt to throw out a base stealer was 1.93 seconds, an AL best.

"I don't know why they run (against Sanchez). It's unbelievable," former Yankees second baseman Starlin

Castro said. "They get a good jump . . . and they get thrown out by two feet."

In some ways, Sanchez breaks the mold of the typical catcher. Often teams prefer a catcher with impeccable defense even if he's not so hot as a hitter. Sanchez is the other way around. And with his power hitting combined with his power arm, he has the ability to be baseball's next great catcher.

"When you're able to put up numbers like he can," Posada said, "he will be."

GARY SANCHEZ AT-A-GLANCE

BIRTHPLACE: Santo Domingo, Dominican Republic

BIRTH DATE: December 2, 1992

POSITION: Catcher

BATS: Right

THROWS: Right

SIZE: 6'2", 230 pounds

TEAM: New York Yankees

MAJOR LEAGUE DEBUT: October 3, 2015 (vs. the Baltimore Orioles)

SIGNED AS AN INTERNATIONAL FREE AGENT BY THE YANKEES IN 2009

CHAPTER 14

COREY SEAGER

Corey Seager's primary motivation isn't to get into the Hall of Fame, hit 500 home runs, or be the best ever.

"My main goal is that I don't want to be bad," the Los Angeles Dodgers' shortstop said. "The accolades and awards are fun, but I'd rather not stink than think about winning an MVP or Rookie of the Year or a Silver Slugger. I just don't want to embarrass myself."

That hasn't been an issue early in Seager's career. Through his first two full major league seasons, the 6-foot-4 shortstop collected two All-Star Game appearances, two Silver Slugger honors, the 2016 NL Rookie of the Year Award, and a top-three finish in NL MVP voting. (His 2018 season, however, was limited to just 26 games by an elbow injury.)

Not stinking at its finest.

The Los Angeles Dodgers' Corey Seager hits a clutch home run in Game 2 of the 2017 World Series.

> **"I THINK WE'VE GROWN TO EXPECT GREATNESS EVERY NIGHT. WHEN HE'S THROWING OUT HITS AND NOT SLUGGING, WE WANT MORE. IT WAS JUST A MATTER OF TIME. IT WAS A SPECIAL NIGHT."**
>
> **—DODGERS MANAGER DAVE ROBERTS**

When asked which Dodgers teammate he admires most, veteran second baseman Chase Utley selected Seager.

"Why?" Utley asked. "Because he's a pretty good player."

The New York Mets found out as much in June 2017. Seager hit not one, not two, but three home runs in a 12–0 Dodgers rout. It was already Seager's second game with three home runs in his career, the first coming in a 2016 win over the Atlanta Braves.

"I think we've grown to expect greatness every night," Dodgers manager Dave Roberts said after Seager's power display against the Mets. "When he's throwing out hits and not slugging, we want more. It was just a matter of time. It was a special night."

Those types of performances aren't going to draw huge reactions out of Seager, who's known for displaying little emotion on the field. That's just not him. Seager described himself as "pretty plain Jane. Pretty vanilla."

"(He's got) an extremely low heart rate," Dodgers third baseman Justin Turner added. "In any situation you don't see him get too up, you don't see him get too down. He's just an even-keeled guy and that's, I think, an advantage in the game of baseball."

But don't let the lack of expression fool you into thinking there's nothing going on upstairs.

"Watching him hit, and watching him play the game, it looks so simple to us," former Dodgers outfielder Trayce Thompson said. "But he's kind of like a duck: on the water he seems cool and collected but in his mind, there's a lot of complex thinking going on."

COREY'S BROTHER

Kyle Seager is no slouch on the diamond. The Seattle infielder made an All-Star game with the Mariners, but he doesn't hold a candle to younger brother Corey, and that's okay with him. On Player's Weekend in 2017, when players had the chance to wear a nickname on the back of their jersey, Kyle chose to sport the name "Corey's brother."

Seager comes from a baseball family. His dad, Jeff, played college baseball. Growing up in Charlotte, North Carolina, Corey and his brothers only watched the New York Yankees, Jeff's favorite team. Just like the Yankees, the Seagers were often pretty successful. One of Corey's brothers, Justin, went on to spend time in the minor leagues. Another brother, Kyle, became an All-Star third baseman for the Seattle Mariners.

Corey was always thinking baseball. That's still true today.

Dodgers manager Dave Roberts said Seager is "as in-tune a young player as I've ever seen."

That shows up at the plate. Seager has established himself as one of the game's top offensive shortstops, capable of hitting for average and power. He's always fine-tuning his swing, paying specific attention to the mechanics and how everything is working together in unison.

"The pace of my mechanics, and all that little stuff that if you're watching the game you don't notice," Seager said. "How the body is working, the pace obviously, the quickness of the (foot) tap, the load back, all that stuff."

Seager's big frame hasn't stopped him from being an outstanding player at shortstop.

Just as much homework goes into his defense. It peeved Seager that people looked at his height and assumed he wouldn't be able to play shortstop.

"That bothered me, because I'm a shortstop," he said.

He's proved as much. Cal Ripken Jr., who sports a similar 6-foot-4 frame, became a Hall of Famer at short, proving it can be done. In Seager, Ripken sees himself.

> "I THOUGHT HIS STYLE WAS A LOT LIKE ME. HE'S FUNDAMENTALLY SOUND. HE'S STRONG IN HIS LOWER HALF. HE'S GOT GOOD FOOTWORK. HE WORKS WELL OFF THE BACKHAND, LIKE I USED TO DO."
>
> —CAL RIPKEN JR.

"I thought his style was a lot like me," Ripken said. "He's fundamentally sound. He's strong in his lower half. He's got good footwork. He works well off the backhand, like I used to do."

And, again, he's smart. He's made plenty of defensive adjustments early in his pro career, from changing his arm slot to taking better routes to balls. Roberts credited Seager for calling the infield coverages that have resulted in the Dodgers turning double plays. Seager said he uses advanced metrics to determine his positioning for specific opposing hitters.

All of those smarts go with his unique set of physical tools. But it's his willingness to adapt to improve that sets him apart.

"He's a student of the game," P. J. Forbes, former manager of the Class Double-A Rancho Cucamonga Quakes, said. "He wants to learn. He asks great questions. He's open to observation. The great thing is he comes to you and you don't have to go to him. That makes it a lot of fun. Obviously, you can see the talent but the way he goes about his work is so professional."

COREY SEAGER AT-A-GLANCE

BIRTHPLACE: Charlotte, North Carolina
BIRTH DATE: April 27, 1994
POSITION: Shortstop
BATS: Left
THROWS: Right
SIZE: 6'4", 220 pounds
TEAM: Los Angeles Dodgers
MAJOR LEAGUE DEBUT: September 3, 2015 (vs. the San Diego Padres)
DRAFTED 18TH OVERALL BY THE LOS ANGELES DODGERS IN 2012

CHAPTER 15

MIKE TROUT

Whether it's a massive home run, a diving catch, or a crafty slide at home, Los Angeles Angels outfielder Mike Trout is the most complete package the baseball world has seen in a long time.

Through his first six complete major league seasons, the Millville, New Jersey, native had six All-Star Game appearances, two AL MVP Awards, and three runner-up finishes in MVP voting. Even in his "worst" season out of the six—a 2017 campaign in which he played just 114 games after dealing with injuries—Trout still finished fourth in the AL MVP race.

Wins Above Replacement is the go-to advanced stat used to evaluate the impact players have on the game. It's defined by Baseball-Reference.com as a "number of wins the player added to the team above

Mike Trout has thrived in all aspects of the game for the Los Angeles Angels.

what a replacement player would add." The "MVP" standard is 8.0. Through 2018, Trout eclipsed 9.0 in five different seasons, going above 10.0 three times.

"If people wanted to build a perfect baseball player in a video game, this is what you'd want your guy to look like," former Angels outfielder Vernon Wells said.

Perfect is an unattainable standard, but Trout might come as close as you can get. He is 6-foot-2, 235 pounds worth of pure baseball goodness. He's the one baseball player who still makes Oakland Athletics executive vice president of baseball operations Billy Beane feel like an eight-year-old kid again.

"I will go to a box score every day to see what he's done," Beane said. "And you've got to go to so many categories that it takes a while."

Trout led the AL in runs scored four times in his first six seasons. Through 2018 he's led the league in walks and on-base percentage three times, and slugging percentage twice. He also led in RBIs and stolen bases once each.

"He is as advertised and is as good as everybody says he is," Angels outfielder Justin Upton said. "When you think of the best player in baseball, you think of a guy who is well-rounded and does everything on the baseball field, and he does that."

Sunday Night Baseball analyst Jessica Mendoza said she would challenge someone watching Trout to "try to find a mistake." And, if you happen to find one, Trout is sure to fix it.

There used to be one solution to getting Trout out—throw him pitches up in the zone. The Kansas City Royals repeatedly threw Trout high pitches in the 2014 ALDS. Trout went 1 for 12 as the Angels were swept in three games. By the following spring, Trout

STAR STRUCK

Trout's favorite baseball player growing up was legendary New York Yankees shortstop Derek Jeter. So when Trout finally had a chance to play against Jeter as a rookie in 2011, he had to make a request. Trout asked Jeter for an autograph. "I think I was on second base when I asked him, 'If I send a ball over, can you sign it?'" Trout said.

Jeter's response is still unknown. "It's like a blur now," Trout said. "I don't even remember what I said because I was so nervous and so star struck."

Three years later, Jeter played in his last All-Star Game. Trout sent him out in style. In the first inning, Jeter got on base with a double. Then Trout tripled to drive Jeter home. Trout ended up being named the game's MVP.

Trout's ability to move quickly allows him to rob home runs like he did against the Seattle Mariners in June 2018.

had erased that weakness. That showed right away in May 2015. He smacked a chest-high fastball from Toronto Blue Jays pitcher Drew Hutchison 412 feet over the center-field fence.

"Now where do you pitch him?" asked Angels bench coach Dino Ebel.

116

The first time Trout felt "fired up on a different level" about a major league achievement came in June 2012. Baltimore Orioles shortstop J. J. Hardy hit a blast on a line to right-center field. The ball was set to sail over the outfield wall by a few feet. But Trout wouldn't let it. He somehow beat the rope to the fence, leaped up, and pulled the ball back, robbing Hardy of a home run. It was one of the few times Trout showed a large amount of emotion. He started to yell, even beating his chest once. Then, he turned around and looked up at the Orioles' video board.

"Had to look up," Trout said. "(I was) standing out there in center field watching the highlight."

Trout has delivered a number defensive plays worth taking a second look at. However, a couple advanced defensive numbers suggested he was below average in the outfield in 2016 and 2017. So at the start of the 2018 season, he made an adjustment. Trout started getting down into his preset defensive position by the time the pitcher released the ball.

"So as soon as contact happens . . . I can make that first jump, as opposed to sitting there for like a half-second, flat-footed," Trout said.

After getting a good jump, Trout's elite speed takes care of the rest. He covers 29.3 feet per second.

"HE'S GOT THE RIGHT MINDSET TO BE SUCCESSFUL FOR A LONG TIME. THAT'S A CHAMPIONSHIP MINDSET."

—ANGELS GENERAL MANAGER, BILLY EPPLER

That kind of giddyap helped him steal 49 bases in 2012. However, his stolen bases dipped to just 11 in 2015. So Trout set a personal goal to be more active, and successful, on the base paths the following season, and swiped 30 bases. Angels general manager Billy Eppler said Trout's commitment to improve is one of his best qualities.

"He's got the right mindset to be successful for a long time," Eppler said. "That's a championship mindset."

Trout's numbers are as gaudy as his highlights are impressive, but former Angels manager Mike Scioscia said to appreciate Trout isn't to focus on the sensational, but rather what he does on a daily basis. But those are often one and the same.

Just look at what Trout did against Toronto in September 2016. Trout was trying to score from second on a sharp single to right field off the bat of Albert Pujols. The throw home by Jose Bautista was on the money and ahead of Trout. No matter, Trout slid well wide of home plate to avoid the tag of Dioner Navarro. Then he slipped his hand in to score just prior to Navarro's glove contacting Trout's armpit.

"That's why he's Mike Trout," Blue Jays pitcher Marcus Stroman said.

"What he does on a daily basis, it's just awesome to watch and be a part of," Angels starter Matt Shoemaker said. "There's always something brand-new he's done in baseball that no one's ever done."

MIKE TROUT AT-A-GLANCE

BIRTHPLACE: Vineland, New Jersey
BIRTH DATE: August 7, 1991
POSITION: Center fielder
BATS: Right
THROWS: Right
SIZE: 6'2", 235 pounds
TEAM: Los Angeles Angels
MAJOR LEAGUE DEBUT: July 8, 2011 (vs. the Seattle Mariners)
DRAFTED 25TH OVERALL BY THE LOS ANGELES ANGELS IN 2009

ROOKIE RECORDS

MOST HOME RUNS

1. Aaron Judge, New York Yankees (2017): 52
2. Mark McGwire, Oakland Athletics (1987): 49
3. Cody Bellinger, Los Angeles Dodgers (2017): 39

MOST HITS

1. Ichiro Suzuki, Seattle Mariners (2001): 242
2. "Shoeless" Joe Jackson, Cleveland Naps (1911): 233
3. Lloyd Waner, Pittsburgh Pirates (1927): 223

MOST STOLEN BASES

1. Billy Hamilton, Kansas City Cowboys (1889): 111
2. Vince Coleman, St. Louis Cardinals (1985): 110
3. Mike Griffin, Baltimore Orioles (1887): 94

MOST PITCHER WINS

1. Larry Corcoran, Chicago White Stockings (1880): 43
T2. Ed Morris, Columbus Buckeyes (1884): 34
T2. Mickey Welch, Troy Trojans (1880): 34

Accurate through the 2018 season

NEW WAVE DREAM TEAM

What might a dream team of players born in 1994 or later look like? Here's what the author says.

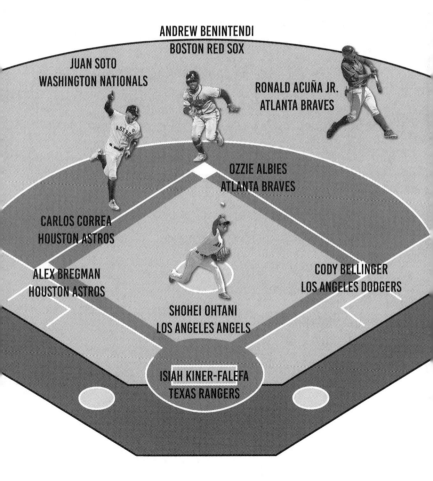

ANDREW BENINTENDI
BOSTON RED SOX

JUAN SOTO
WASHINGTON NATIONALS

RONALD ACUÑA JR.
ATLANTA BRAVES

OZZIE ALBIES
ATLANTA BRAVES

CARLOS CORREA
HOUSTON ASTROS

ALEX BREGMAN
HOUSTON ASTROS

CODY BELLINGER
LOS ANGELES DODGERS

SHOHEI OHTANI
LOS ANGELES ANGELS

ISIAH KINER-FALEFA
TEXAS RANGERS

FOR MORE INFORMATION

BOOKS

Kuenster, Robert. *Baseball's Top 10: Ranking the Best Major League Players by Position.* Lanham, MD: Rowman & Littlefield, 2015.

Rausch, David. *Major League Baseball.* Minneapolis: Bellwether Media, Inc., 2015.

Schuh, Mari. *Stars of Baseball.* North Mankato, MN: Capstone Press, 2014.

ON THE WEB

Baseball Prospectus
www.baseballprospectus.com

Baseball Reference
www.baseball-reference.com

Major League Baseball
www.mlb.com

PLACES TO VISIT

National Baseball Hall of Fame and Museum
25 Main Street
Cooperstown, NY 13326
888-425-5663
www.baseballhall.org

The game's greatest players are enshrined in the Hall of Fame. Visitors can tour the museum and learn about the players and baseball history in general through interactive exhibits.

Negro Leagues Baseball Museum
1616 East 18th Street
Kansas City, MO 64108
816-221-1920
www.nlbm.com

Located in Kansas City, which was at the center of the Negro Leagues, this museum honors the great players who were for many years kept out of the major leagues due to their skin color.

SELECT BIBLIOGRAPHY

Carelli, Christopher. "SN50: Carlos Correa's Meteoric Rise Is Hardly a Surprise." *Sporting News*, Sept. 2017, www.sportingnews.com/us/mlb/news/sn-50-best-mlb-players-carlos-correa-astros-stats-fantasy/156fd3c4q0fh61iq0l5rmckv4t.

Keown, Tim. "Going against the Grind." *ESPN The Magazine*, June 2017, www.espn.com/espn/feature/story/_/id/19591088/baltimore-orioles-manny-machdo-face-mlb-new-identity?ex_cid=espnapi_public.

Keown, Tim. "Sorry Not Sorry." *ESPN The Magazine*, March 2016, www.espn.com/espn/feature/story/_/id/14935765/washington-nationals-bryce-harper-wants-change-baseball-forever.

Kilgore, Adam. "A Swing of Beauty." *Washington Post*, May 2013, www.washingtonpost.com/wp-srv/special/sports/bryce-harper-swing-of-beauty/.

Nusbaum, Eric. "How Corey Seager Became One of Baseball's Best-Hitting Shortstops." *Vice Sports*, March 2017, www.sports.vice.com/en_us/article/xybnkd/how-corey-seager-became-one-of-baseballs-best-hitting-shortstops.

Ortiz, Jorge L. "Houston Astros' Alex Bregman Is USA TODAY Sports' Minor League Player of the Year." *USA Today*, Sept. 2016, www.usatoday.com/story/sports/mlb/2016/09/06/houston-astros-alex-bregman-minor-league-player-year/89912660/.

Rosenthal, Ken. "With Shohei Ohtani, the Beauty Is in the Mystery, the Magic Is in the Promise." *The Athletic*, 4 April 2018, www.theathletic.com/315702/2018/04/15/with-shohei-ohtani-the-beauty-is-in-the-mystery-the-magic-is-in-the-promise/.

Verducci, Tom. "Born to Win: Is the Kris Bryant Story Too Good to Be True? No, but the Cubs Will Take It." *Sports Illustrated*, March 2017, www.si.com/mlb/2017/03/21/kris-bryant-chicago-cubs-born-win.

INDEX

ABOUT THE AUTHOR

Jace Frederick is a sports reporter for the St. Paul *Pioneer Press* in Minnesota, where he covers high school sports and the NBA's Minnesota Timberwolves. A native of western Wisconsin, Frederick graduated with a journalism degree from the University of Minnesota and now resides in nearby Mounds View. *Baseball's New Wave* is his first book.